LifeCaps Presents:

The Golden Genius:

The Amazing Life of Maria Altmann

By Fergus Mason

BookCaps™ Study Guides

www.bookcaps.com

Cover Image © Mike-Fotografie – Fotolia

Table of Contents

About LifeCaps

LifeCaps is an imprint of BookCaps™ Study Guides. With each book, a lesser known or sometimes forgotten life is recapped. We publish a wide array of topics (from baseball and music to literature and philosophy), so check our growing catalogue regularly (**www.bookcaps.com**) to see our newest books.

Introduction: The Auction

It was no surprise the painting was the most talked-about item in Christie's catalog. Its appearance alone is striking enough. A sea of gold leaf surrounds a finely detailed, stylized portrait of a pouting, dark-haired woman. Some of the gold is interwoven with intricate painted patterns; more is applied over a rough layer of glue, then lightly buffed to leave it sparkling with highlights. Only the woman's face and hands show any attempt at realism. Most of the canvas looks, at first glance, to be a random assortment of shapes. Take a longer look, however, and order begins to emerge from the golden chaos. The woman's dress comes into view, subtly different from the bright swirl that surrounds it. The jagged contrasts that first catch the eye resolve into a coherent image. It's not a painting you could walk past as you explored a gallery – it's just too vivid for that. It's also very obviously the work of Gustav Klimt, from his "golden phase" in the first decade of the 20th century.

Klimt's most significant paintings don't come on the market very often, so given his continuing popularity this sale was always going to generate a lot of excitement, but there was more to the art cognoscenti's gossip than the mere fact it was on offer. The painting - *Portrait of Adele Bloch-Bauer I* – had a complicated story behind it. The circumstances that had brought it to the famous London-based auctioneers formed a tangled web involving Klimt's private life, the glittering heights of pre-war Viennese society, the Nazis and an international legal battle. Now, a 90-year-old woman, the niece of the painting's subject, had asked Christie's New York office to sell it for her.

The painting's owner, Austrian-American Maria Altmann, had never set out to cause a controversy. She'd just wanted to recover some property that had been stolen from her family decades earlier, in one of the darkest periods of European history. What actually happened brought the spotlight of publicity onto how many of the finest paintings in European galleries came to be there, and gave many others hope of finally reclaiming their own belongings from the accidental beneficiaries of the Nazis' greed. Born in the Austro-Hungarian Empire during the First World War, Altmann's life took in many changes in her country of birth. One of those changes sent her to a new life in the USA; others were more positive. Altmann watched most of them from far away in California, in her adopted country. Finally, however, she set out to right an old wrong and engaged with the Austrian government – a process that ended up in the US Supreme Court.

Chapter 1: The Golden Genius

To understand why Maria Altmann's life followed the course it did we need to go back to Vienna, decades before she was even born.

Gustav Klimt was born in Baumgarten, near Vienna, in 1862. His father was a gold engraver and the entire family had a strong interest in art, so Klimt enrolled at Vienna's School of Arts And Crafts in the mid-1870s. His younger brother Ernst joined him there in 1877 and by 1880 the brothers, along with Franz Matsch, were taking commissions for murals and portrait work. By 1888, Klimt had been given an award by the Austro-Hungarian emperor for his work on public murals and was one of central Europe's best known painters. Then, in 1892, his father and his brother Ernst both died, and he found himself responsible for supporting their families.

Klimt's artistic talents covered a wide range, but the most profitable work available was in painting portraits for rich patrons. To pay for his new responsibilities he concentrated more on this market, and soon became one of the most sought-after portrait painters in Austria. His works were unconventional and heavily stylized, rather than the realist style traditionally used for portraits, and in the first decade of the 20th century he began what's now known as his "Golden Phase". Drawing on his father's familiarity with gold, he began to use gold leaf in large quantities. Gold leaf is a very versatile material that can be easily textured. The sheets of metal are so thin that they take on the texture of the background they're glued to, so by preparing the canvas with textured paint before applying the leaf it can be given different appearances, and then buffed once the glue has dried. Combined with vividly colored paint the technique let Klimt create extremely striking images that were soon immensely popular with his clients.

Most of those clients were female, and Klimt himself turned out to be quite popular with several of them. The painter was an active member of Vienna's "Bohemian" scene, a subculture populated by artists and writers. In Klimt's case the phrase had a double meaning; his father actually did come from the old Kingdom of Bohemia, in what's now the Czech Republic, but the term had come to mean the unconventional, often socially permissive, lifestyle followed by many creative people and their hangers-on. Turn of the century Austria was a very conservative society, dominated by the imperial aristocracy and the Catholic Church; Klimt had already faced criticism for "pornographic" art. It's true that many of his paintings featured some nudity, but they certainly weren't pornographic. Perhaps because of the controversy generated by his work he was very careful to keep his private life discreet, but it was nevertheless colorful.

In 1891 Ernst Klimt met and married Helene Flöge; when Ernst died the next year Gustav Klimt became her legal guardian. Through her he met her sister Emilie, then 18 years old, and the two began a relationship that lasted the rest of Klimt's life. There's still debate about whether it was ever a sexual relationship, although many art experts cite Klimt's painting *The Kiss*, for which Flöge modeled, as evidence that it was. It was certainly a close one; Klimt's last words before his death were "Get Emilie" and she inherited half his estate.[i] Flöge was a fashion designer, noted for her often revolutionary styles, and Klimt often helped her out with sketches. He became close to her family, and from 1893 onwards spent his summers with them at their vacation home by the Attersee Lake. For Klimt it was an opening into the richer layers of society; the artist himself was still living in a small apartment with his mother and two of his sisters.[ii] The relationship was a tempestuous one, though. Vienna society might not know about Klimt's numerous affairs, but Emilie did and she was often infuriated. Once, after Klimt was caught with Alma Schindler, she considered suicide. Finally she visited psychoanalysis pioneer Sigmund Freud, who predictably diagnosed Klimt as being obsessed with his mother and suggested she leave him. She didn't; instead she developed her work as a distraction and put up with his womanizing as best she could.

One of the women with whom Klimt was repeatedly linked was Adele Bloch-Bauer. Her husband Ferdinand Bloch was a wealthy industrialist who had inherited a successful sugar refining business. In 1899, aged 35, he met and married the 18-year-old Adele Bauer. Adele's own family was also wealthy; her father was a bank president. Between them the couple had enough money to live an extravagant lifestyle and they used much of it to support their favorite causes. Ferdinand disliked the rulers of the Austro-Hungarian Empire and channeled part of his wealth to Social Democrat politicians, including Karl Renner who later became the first president of the Austrian republic. He also encouraged writers, such as Stefan Zweig, and artists. Klimt soon became a favorite of his. Meanwhile, Adele began running a regular salon, a series of meetings where artists and enthusiasts could socialize. Klimt was also a frequent guest at these events. Soon, Adele began to visit his studio.

One of Klimt's best known paintings is *Judith and the Head of Holofernes*, based on the Biblical story of how Judith seduced then decapitated the Babylonian general. The revealingly dressed figure of Judith bears a strong resemblance to Adele. *Judith* was painted in 1901 and includes significant amounts of gold leaf, although the actual Golden Phase was yet to come. Then in 1907, Klimt was commissioned to paint a portrait of Adele herself, rather than using her as a model for another subject.

There was gold in *Judith*, but in *Portrait of Adele Bloch-Bauer I* the yellow metal ran riot across the canvas. Klimt started by painting Adele's face – with a similar expression to the one she wore in *Judith* – in a semi-realistic style. Then he surrounded it with a few highly stylized elements – her dress, and hints of a baseboard and green carpet – and filled the rest of the picture with textured and embellished gold. Around her face is a field of painted and embossed disks and spirals that evokes images of planets and galaxies. The effect is almost religious, despite the lack of any overt religious imagery. Many art critics think it's the defining work of his Golden Phase. It was also among the last he did in that style – possibly his final work that made extensive use of gold, in fact.[iii]

Klimt took three years to complete the portrait, although of course he worked on other commissions at the same time. When it was completed it went into Ferdinand Bloch's private collection, although as a patron of the arts he regularly loaned his paintings to exhibitions. When it wasn't on display to the public it usually hung in his bedroom.

For the elite of Viennese society a Klimt portrait was a highly desirable status symbol, one that you couldn't necessarily get just by being wealthy. Sometimes a wealthy client would offer a commission and be accepted; sometimes he would be declined. Meanwhile Klimt painted portraits of piano teachers and a bar owner's daughter. To get a Klimt portrait of yourself, your wife or daughter took more than just money; it also needed a social connection to the artist himself. And just to increase the scarcity value even more, he never did more than one portrait of the same person – except for Adele Bloch-Bauer.

In 1912 Klimt painted a second portrait of Adele, in a very different style. There was no gold leaf this time, and although the image was still heavily stylized it was more conventional in many ways. The face, again, is the most realistic element and is very similar to both the first portrait and *Judith*. Once more it's given a religious effect by Adele's hat, which resembles a halo. The fact he'd chosen to do two portraits of Adele caused some speculation about the relationship between artist and subject, even though Klimt was still being as discreet about his many affairs as he could. In fact it's believed he fathered as many as fourteen children by various lovers between 1891 and 1908. Even when people suspected Klimt of an affair, though, it was usually glossed over. By this time he'd established himself as one of the leading lights of the Viennese art scene, and for such a prominent artist many things could be forgiven or ignored.

His popularity gave Klimt a privileged position in Vienna's crowded artistic scene. He was able to afford a spacious studio, where he worked in a casual atmosphere – he usually painted wearing just sandals and a simple loose robe. His rich clients allowed him comfort and privacy. Others had to make do with much less. When Klimt painted the first portrait of Adele, another painter, 27 years younger than him, was living in a cramped hostel in Vienna's Mariahilf district and scratching a meager living selling watercolors to tourists. Twice rejected by the Vienna Academy of Fine Art for insufficient talent,[iv] he finally gave up and moved to Munich in 1913. When the First World War broke out a year later he returned to Austria and tried to join the army, but was rejected on medical grounds. Undaunted, he went back to Munich again and joined the Bavarian Army – part of the semi-federal Imperial German Army – instead. Perhaps the Bavarians were less choosy or perhaps they felt such a keen volunteer deserved a chance. Perhaps they were right.

Four years later, the young man's commander, *Leutnant* Hugo Gutmann, successfully recommended him for the Iron Cross First Class – a decoration rarely awarded to low-ranking soldiers like Lance Corporal Hitler.

Chapter 2: Vienna

Hitler's world of struggling would-be painters was part of the Bohemian art scene that thrived in Vienna, but it was a long way from the circles Klimt moved in. The future Nazi dictator always claimed he'd developed his loathing of Jews in Vienna, but several historians dispute that. In fact there's strong evidence that he had friends among the poor Czech and Ukrainian Jews who made up a large part of the artistic population.[v] If he was an anti-Semite before Germany's defeat in 1918 he hid it well – *Leutnant* Gutmann, who admired Hitler's courage enough to recommend him for a medal usually only given to officers, was Jewish.

In Eastern Europe Jews were mostly poor and confined to ghettoes; in Western Europe they tended to be found among the middle and upper classes. In Vienna, a thoroughly Central European city, they were represented in every rank of society in considerable numbers – by the beginning of the 20th century almost 9 percent of the city's population was Jewish. The Bloch family was definitely towards the higher end of the scale and both Ferdinand and his brother were expected to find suitable wives of an appropriate rank in the community. As it turned out the two brothers married two sisters: Gustav Bloch married Adele's sister Therese, who also changed her name to Bloch-Bauer on marriage. The two marriages formed a close link between the two families that was to have a huge influence on later events.

Klimt was notable for the number of illegitimate children he fathered, but if he did have an affair with Adele she didn't get pregnant as a result. She didn't have any children with Ferdinand either, however, and the couple remained childless. The same didn't apply to Gustav and Therese. They had five children, including Adele's niece Maria.

Maria Viktoria Bloch was born in Vienna on February 18, 1916. It was a troubled time; the Austro-Hungarian Empire had been at war for two years and things weren't going all that well. Serbia had been defeated, but at the cost of more than a quarter of a million troops. There was a stalemate in the south where Italian and Austrian armies battered away at each other, slowly bleeding the empire's forces. In the east Russian pressure was steadily increasing – by the end of the year another million soldiers would be dead in Russia. Romania declared war on the empire in August and invaded Hungary; they were driven out again, and Romania's own capital captured, but that campaign tied up even more men. With their German allies bogged down in bloody trench warfare in France the war was not turning out to be the swift triumph Vienna had expected in 1914.

Nevertheless, life in Vienna went on pleasantly enough. The Blochs and Bauers were part of the social elite, so they didn't face conscription. The war also made Ferdinand Blochs's business more important. The family involvement in the sugar trade was begun by Ferdinand's father David Bloch, but Ferdinand himself expanded the small family firm into a much larger and more profitable one. *Österreichische Zuckerindustrie* AG (Austrian Sugar Industry), usually known as ÖZAG, was founded on August 6, 1909 to capitalize on the growing trade in sugar beet. Sugar had been an expensive luxury in Europe until the middle of the 18th century, and even after that the supply was far from reliable. The main source of sugar was from sugar cane, and most of the world's supply came from the Caribbean and India – in other words it was controlled by Britain. When the Napoleonic Wars broke out at the end of the 18th century sugar supplies to continental Europe immediately fell away to a trickle from the much smaller empire of the Netherlands, and within weeks a blockade by the Royal Navy had closed that off too. In response, France developed new techniques to extract sugar from sugar beet, which unlike cane would grow in Europe. By the early 20th century selective breeding had raised the sucrose content of beets from 5 or 6 percent to around 20 percent, and most of Europe's sugar came from domestic beet crops. Only Britain continued to rely on imported cane sugar, and even there the new varieties were growing in popularity. Germany and Austria, with their heavy damp soil, were ideal for growing sugar beet and the industry flourished. ÖZAG quickly prospered, and the demand for high-energy military rations during the war did the business no harm at all.

Meanwhile, Gustav Bloch was building a successful career as an attorney. He had married Therese on March 22, 1898, at the age of 35. By that time he was already well established in his legal practice, and for a while it probably looked as if he would make more money than his brother Ferdinand. He and his young wife (Therese was 23 when they married) had their first child, Karl, in April 1901. By the end of 1907 they had four, three sons and a baby daughter.

With two brothers married to two sisters it's not surprising that the couples were very close, and the childless Ferdinand and Adele doted on Gustav and Therese's children. They took them out almost every Sunday, and spent long periods with them each summer.[vi] That continued after the war broke out – none of the three boys were old enough to face conscription and with aerial bombing in its infancy the fighting had no direct impact on Vienna. The number of young men fell as they were conscripted into the army but for most people life went on. Luxuries became scarce and taxes rose, but people still needed lawyers and sugar. The Bloch-Bauers continued to prosper, especially Ferdinand and Adele. Then, nine years after the birth of their fourth child, Gustav and Therese unexpectedly had a fifth: Maria.

When Maria was born in February 1916 the war hadn't yet swung decisively against Austria-Hungary and the mood was still quite optimistic, but that slowly changed. It became obvious that the empire's generals had been promoted for their connections to the royal family, not for their military competence. The Germans increasingly took command of Austrian troops. At the same time Hungary, the home of most of the empire's agriculture, had its own issues and food deliveries to Austria became less reliable. The people began to grow restless. As early as late 1916 the leadership started trying to negotiate a separate peace with their enemies, the Triple Entente of Britain, France and Russia. The Entente powers, furious about Austria's support of Germany, refused. At the same time Germany was increasingly impatient with their unreliable ally; some German generals described the alliance as being like "shackled to a corpse". Across the empire nationalist movements began to grow, as minorities – Croats, Slovenes, even many Hungarians – became ever more resentful of Austria's dominance.

As the German and Austro-Hungarian armies were slowly ground down by constant combat and the USA finally entered the war it became obvious they were going to lose. A last German offensive on the Western Front threatened to tip the balance for a while, but when it failed, the end of the war was inevitable. Italy launched a new offensive in spring of 1918 that the Austro-Hungarian Army was barely able to resist. Taking advantage of the chaos, expatriate Czechs and Slovaks in the USA began planning a new country on the territory of the Kingdom of Bohemia; on October 18 they declared Czechoslovakia independent and the breakup of the empire began. The Croats and South Slavs broke away to form what would later become Yugoslavia. Then on October 31, the Hungarian Prime Minister, Mihály Károlyi, officially terminated his country's relationship with Austria. That was the end of the Austro-Hungarian Empire. Three days later, with the British, French and Italians advancing from the south and the remains of the army collapsing, the leaders of both Austria and Hungary signed a general armistice with the Allies. Germany surrendered on November 11, ending the war and starting a chain of events that changed the map of Europe.

Austria had been part of the empire, and Vienna the more important of its joint capitals, since 1867; before that it had ruled the same territory alone. Suddenly it found itself stripped of its satellite states, all of which were independent by the end of 1918. Its internal politics had changed too. The royal family lost power and the country became a republic, with left- and right-wing factions struggling for power. It was also in a very weak position internationally. The victorious Entente powers took a hard line in the post-armistice negotiations aimed at securing a permanent peace; France was particularly vindictive. Through 1919 Austria saw more and more of its land stripped away and attached to neighboring states – the Sudetenland went to Czechoslovakia, parts of Tyrol to Italy and various other small "adjustments". The end result of the process was a mess; many of the new states, and regions that had been transferred to other countries, were still tied into the Viennese banking system. So many changes in a short space of time left society anxious and unsettled, and the political scene reflected that.

Austrian politics in the republic's first decades spread across the whole spectrum, from Marxist revolutionaries inspired by the newly founded Soviet Union to the extreme right wing. Some representatives in the new parliament wanted to nationalize all businesses and turn the country into a workers' state. Others, now that the Czech and Serbo-Croat speaking regions had left to form their own nations, wanted to unify German-speaking Austria with Germany itself. The political process wasn't always a peaceful one and street battles were common. An extreme right-wing militia, the *Heimwehr*, had started to come together not long after the war. Most of its members were former soldiers and strongly nationalistic. In response the leftist Social Democratic Workers' Party formed its own militia, the *Republikanischer Schutzbund* (Republican Protection League), again mostly from demobilized soldiers. There were many other militias, most of them small and short-lived, but these two were both powerful forces in Austrian politics through the 1920s and early

1930s.

It was an uncomfortable situation. The conservative Christian Social Party soon began to dominate politics, and from 1920 on every chancellor of Austria belonged to it. The main opposition was the Social Democrats and that left families like the Bloch-Bauers stuck awkwardly in the middle. Central European Jews have traditionally tended to be moderately left-wing, but as well-off industrialists and lawyers the Bloch-Bauers didn't agree with ideas like nationalization of industry or the forced redistribution of wealth. Economically they had far more in common with the Christian Social Party, but they didn't want anything to do with the CS and the CS didn't want anything to do with them. The problem was that while it was economically right wing the party was also closely linked to the Catholic church, which was still promoting anti-Semitism at the time. To increase its support in the countryside the CS increasingly played up its religious element and dislike of Jews became more open as time passed. For families like the Bloch-Bauers it usually seemed safer to just stay out of politics. Of course, there was no urgent need to get involved. The chaos of the empire's collapse had created plenty of work for lawyers, so Gustav had a huge pool of legal work to choose from. In fact, he preferred to concentrate on art, and spent most of his time cataloguing and expanding Ferdinand's collections of paintings and porcelain.

Meanwhile, Ferdinand's sugar company had been largely unaffected by the war, and was supplying more than 20 percent of Austria's sugar. Things weren't quite as good as they'd once been but they were still part of Vienna's social and financial elite. Ferdinand's art collection was by now one of the best in Austria and contained five paintings by Klimt, including one of his last works (the artist died on February 6, 1918). As long as they didn't attract the attention of either left- or right-wing mobs their comfortable life continued much as it had before. The families mingled with other well-off Viennese, and as the children reached their twenties the search for suitable spouses began. Then tragedy struck.

Meningitis is a disease that causes inflammation of the membranes protecting the brain and spinal cord. Before antibiotics were introduced in the 1930s more than 90 percent of victims died, and even today it's a very dangerous condition. It may have been known to doctors as far back as ancient Greece but epidemics became more common in the mid-19th century. It was an Austrian, Anton Weichselbaum, who in 1887 identified the bacteria that could cause meningitis. Decades later penicillin proved effective against this bacteria, but in 1925 penicillin hadn't even be discovered yet, and there was little that could be done for meningitis sufferers except to keep them comfortable and hope their immune system could bring down the swelling in time. In January 1925, when Maria was nine, Adele Bloch-Bauer began complaining of serious headaches and a stiff neck. Then she succumbed to a sudden fever, and meningitis was diagnosed. The Bloch-Bauers could afford the best doctors in Vienna but nothing worked and Adele's condition swiftly deteriorated. On

January 24 she died.

The wills of the wealthy often turn out to be complex, with unpredictable and far-reaching implications, and Adele's was no exception. Most of its contents were uncontroversial but one point was going to have effects, impossible to predict in 1924, that would echo for more than eight decades. Adele had always loved her husband's collection of Klimt paintings, especially the two portraits of herself, and she hated the thought of them one day being inherited by people they had no personal meaning for. In her will she asked her husband to revise his own will so that, on his death, the paintings would be donated to the Austrian State Gallery.

Adele's request made sense. The *Österreichische Galerie*, which since 1921 has been housed in the spectacular Belvedere Palace, is one of the finest art collections in the world. More to the point it already housed two of Klimt's most popular works, *Judith* and *The Kiss*. Both of these make heavy use of gold and their style is similar to the first portrait of Adele, and it was natural for an art lover to want all three to hang together.

The problem was that Adele didn't own the paintings – Ferdinand did. If life had carried on as before there's an excellent chance that Ferdinand would have honored his wife's request and donated his Klimts to the Belvedere, possibly on his own death or even before, but a request was all it was. It didn't put him under any legal obligation to make the donation and it certainly didn't give the State Gallery any claim on the works. That fact was to become very significant later but in 1924, amid the trauma of Adele's death, it passed almost unnoticed. For now the paintings stayed in Ferdinand's Vienna mansion, with the portraits of Adele hanging in his bedroom to watch over him.

For Gustav, Therese and their children family life went on. The first of the children to marry was their second son, Leopold. In 1929 he married Antoinette Pick, well known for her skills on horseback, and their son Peter was born the following year. Ferdinand's business grew into one of Austria's top sugar producers, Gustav practiced law and the remaining children found their places among the Viennese elite. Austria's political tensions never went away, but slowly they calmed. What nobody could foresee was that events across the border would soon shatter Vienna's sophisticated society beyond repair.

Chapter 3: Nazism

Austria had lost an empire and a ruling imperial family after the war, but slowly achieved the transition to a much smaller republic. To the north, however, Germany was a powder keg and there were plenty of sparks fizzing around it. It was Austria-Hungary's actions in the Balkans that had dragged the Central Powers into war, but in the end, Germany's powerful military had done the most damage to the Triple Entente and the French were out for revenge. Most of the fighting on the Western Front had taken place in France and significant areas of the country had been devastated; more to the point the reputation of the "invincible" French army had been ground brutally into the mud. For a nation as touchy and obsessed with national pride as the French that was unforgivable and they set out to punish Germany as severely as they could.

The Treaty of Versailles, which turned the November 1918 armistice into a formal peace, was aimed at forcing Germany to take full responsibility for the war then making her compensate the western allies for the cost. Britain and the USA were lukewarm about this; the British knew that blame for the war was more complex than that. The English-speaking allies were also worried about the consequences. They felt that while the harsh measures demanded by France could cripple Germany in the short term, eventually she would recover – and was likely to be in a vengeful mood when she did so. The British may also have been reluctant to build up a traditional enemy – France – at the cost of a traditional ally, and pushed for much weaker sanctions. The USA didn't support punishing Germany at all, and felt (rightly) that making Europe prosperous would do more to prevent war than trying to destroy its most powerful economy.

However the French insisted, and Germany was ordered to pay a series of humiliating penalties. Parts of the country were handed over to France, Poland and Denmark. The French forced Berlin to demilitarize the Rhineland, the area between the German border and the Rhine River – a strip of land that in places was a hundred miles wide. Germany was ordered to pay reparations – mostly to France – in cash, ships and industrial facilities that totaled around $5 billion (more than $1 *trillion* in 2014 dollars).

Militarily, Germany was forbidden to have tanks, other armored vehicles, chemical weapons or military aircraft. There was also a ban on researching or manufacturing these weapons even if they weren't put into service. The navy was limited to a handful of obsolete battleships (the treaty specified that these had to be pre-*Dreadnought* designs, and the launch of HMS *Dreadnought* in 1905 had made every older battleship irrelevant) and a few cruisers and destroyers. Submarines were forbidden. There was to be no air force of any kind. Finally, the army was limited to 100,000 men and the feared General Staff was dissolved. Then the French made a mistake. They were worried that Germany would be able to build up a large pool of trained manpower by funneling men through the army quickly, so they insisted that conscription be banned. More rules demanded that enlisted men had to serve for at least twelve years, and officers for at least 25. The German generals protested bitterly about this, but inside they weren't as reluctant as they seemed – they could see possibilities that the French had overlooked.

Overall the Treaty left Germany weakened, almost bankrupt and virtually defenseless – with no tanks or air force they had no hope of repelling an invasion by modern forces. The French troops in the Rhineland looted the region ruthlessly, stripping factories of their machinery and seizing all the railway rolling stock they could get their hands on. The resentment this generated was incredible. The French army had failed miserably at holding back the Germans, and without British and later US assistance would inevitably have collapsed; now French troops were strutting round western Germany like pillaging conquerors. That humiliation alone was almost unbearable. But it was being shoveled on top of an even deeper, more dangerous resentment.

Germany was defeated in the First World War. By 1918, the economy was on the verge of collapse and most of the population was sick of the war's unbelievable human cost. Even the army was slowly falling apart; although its best units were superbly trained and highly effective, many divisions were suffering badly from desertion and low morale. The Hundred Days Offensive from August-November 1918 drove the majority of the German army out of France and killed, wounded or captured more than a million men. If the war hadn't been ended by the armistice, Germany itself would have been overrun in 1919. However, the guns had barely fallen silent when a myth began to spread that the army had been betrayed – the "stab in the back" – by the civilian government, especially the revolutionaries who had forced the Kaiser to stand down in favor of a republican government on November 9, 1918.

It was pressure from the leftist Social Democratic Party that imposed a republic on Germany after the revolution, but that hadn't been the original plan. The revolution was spearheaded by extreme left groups, including the Spartacus League, the Free Workers' Union and the Bavarian Soviet Republic. These were internationalist Marxist groups and their leaders had close links with the leaders of the new Soviet regime. Their leaders were also, to a very large extent, Jewish. And there were plenty disgruntled right-wingers ready to jump on that fact.

Austria had its left- and right-wing militias, but Germany had much larger ones on both sides and the most powerful of these was the *Freikorps*. It began as groups of former soldiers, mostly still in uniform and often carrying their service weapons, who formed up to defend their communities against political rioters. Before long it had become a loose network of anticommunist paramilitary groups who covered the political spectrum from Social Democrat to the far right. The *Freikorps* was used by the Social Democrats to put down the most extreme revolutionaries – Spartacist leaders Karl Liebknecht and Rosa Luxemburg were executed by the *Freikorps* in Berlin on January 15, 1919.

The unrest gradually subsided as the post-war government transitioned into the Weimar Republic, but Germany was never fully at peace. The *Freikorps* and other militias faded away but many of their members gravitated to extremist political parties. There were many of these groups, most of them small and chaotic. Some of them worried the government though, and one of those was the DAP – the *Deutsche Arbeiterpartei*, or German Worker's Party. In fact, it worried them enough that they decided to put an agent inside it and started looking around for a suitable candidate. Eventually they settled on a decorated NCO who, fearing unemployment, was fighting desperately to stay in the shrinking army. He was transferred to a reconnaissance unit of the *Reichswehr* and sent to infiltrate the DAP. Unfortunately, the army hadn't considered the possibility that their agent would be impressed by the DAP's eccentric mix of nationalism, anti-capitalism and "non-Jewish" socialism. They were also unaware that the corporal had a gift for public speaking, which was spectacularly demonstrated at a party meeting in a Munich beer hall on September 12, 1919. A heckler criticized the DAP's opposition to capitalism and suggested that Bavaria should secede from the largely Protestant north of Germany and form a new, Catholic, nation with Austria. The *Reichswehr* agent delivered a passionate speech that demolished the heckler's arguments and drew enthusiastic applause from the DAP leadership. Days later the party leader, Anton Drexler, personally invited him to join the party.[vii] The army agent was Adolf Hitler.

In February 1920, in an effort to increase its appeal, the party added "Nationalsozialistische" in front of its name. Hitler, who had already become the party's chief of propaganda, preferred "Social Revolutionary Party" but was persuaded to go with NSDAP. In any case a new, informal name soon came into use. The German language is very good at generating extremely long and complex multisyllable words. The German people are just as good at reducing them to short, snappy abbreviations, especially when it's a political party they don't like. The Social Democrats were already referred to as *Sozis* by their opponents. Within months the new party had a similar nickname – Nazis.

The Nazi party grew through the early 1920s, campaigning on a platform of extreme nationalism, nationalization of industry and an expansion of social welfare programs. Hitler was elected party leader on June 28, 1921 and that boosted the Nazis even more; Drexler was a railway worker and poet, while Hitler was a decorated veteran who could appeal to the millions of ex-soldiers in Germany. At the same time the party attracted support from the unemployed, small businessmen struggling with punitive interest rates and the ultra-nationalist right. It never came close to winning a place in government, though, and Hitler's ambition led him to look for other ways to get power. Then, in October 1922, Mussolini's National Fascist party seized control of Italy by launching an audacious coup that relied on popular support and intimidation rather than direct violence. The disciplined Fascists, with their straight-arm Roman salute and paramilitary uniforms, impressed Hitler; he started looking for an excuse to follow their example.

In 1923 it came. Germany, struggling under runaway inflation, couldn't meet its reparations payments and in retaliation France invaded and occupied the Ruhrgebiet. With its industrial heartland controlled by French troops and the raw materials the economy needed being seized as reparations, Germany collapsed into near-chaos. The communists attempted to launch a revolution, which failed but persuaded 20,000 more Germans to join the Nazis. Emboldened, Hitler launched his own coup on November 8 and it failed miserably. The army refused to support him, sixteen Nazis were shot dead by the police and the party was banned in retaliation. Hitler spent a year in jail. When he was released he managed to reform and reorganize the party in a new, legal form, and tried again to win power legally. He was no more successful than the last time and the party was doing well to get 4 percent of the vote in national elections. Then came the Great Depression.

The Depression was hard in the USA. In Germany it was a catastrophe, and the main parties seemed helpless to do anything about it. The Germans were suddenly willing to listen to alternatives and by the end of 1930 the Nazi vote had jumped to 18.3 percent. Over the next two years that almost doubled and new elections in November 1932 gave them 33.1 percent, by far the largest party. The other parties failed to form a coalition that could keep him out of office and on January 30, 1933 President Hindenburg appointed Hitler as chancellor of Germany.

Within weeks of being appointed Hitler had managed to persuade the president to suspend most civil liberties, allow him to pass laws without a parliamentary vote and ban many of the other parties. Then he used these dictatorial powers to rebuild Germany. The economy was restructured, huge public works programs created jobs and the infrastructure was modernized. With the Depression receding the Nazi policies quickly brought unemployment down and stabilized the currency, making Hitler immensely popular. But he was also, first quietly then more openly, tearing up the military restrictions of Versailles. New designs for tanks and combat aircraft were being secretly tested in Russia thanks to a deal with Stalin. "Experimental" submarines started operating in the Baltic. And a huge expansion of the army was planned.

In theory, the Versailles rules should have left Germany with a small army suitable only for limited defense. In practice, given 100,000 long-service regulars to command, the generals had turned the *Reichswehr* into a huge leadership academy. The officer and NCO schools weren't teaching their students the duties of the ranks they held; they were training them to occupy a position *three grades higher*. Every rifleman was a potential squad leader, corporals could lead companies and majors knew how to handle a division. The generals who commanded this force of less than a dozen divisions were learning grand strategy that would let them maneuver massive army groups. The General Staff might have been disbanded but its members had managed to create and train the command structure for a force twenty times larger than the one Germany was allowed. By the late 1930s the renamed *Wehrmacht* was growing rapidly, and had already become one of the best equipped and most powerful armies in Europe. Now Hitler was looking for someone to unleash it against.

A central plank of Nazi policy had always been racial solidarity and the unification of the entire "German people" as one nation. The border changes that followed Versailles had left German minorities in many countries, most notably Poland, Czechoslovakia and France, and Hitler had plans for those. But first he wanted to go for an easier target, a largely pro-German country where the Nazi party already had considerable support: Austria.

Chapter 4: The Anschluss

The rise of Nazism in Germany added a new and dangerous element to Austria's simmering political tensions and the conservative government, under pressure from both left and right, began restricting political activity in an attempt to keep the administration running. Socialist violence broke out in February 1934 and had to be suppressed by the army, then in July the Austrian Nazis attempted a coup. Again the army defeated it, and thirteen leading Nazis were executed. Evidence suggested that instructions for the coup had come from Hitler's regime in Germany, but that there was considerable support from inside Austria itself.

However, most of the political violence was happening in the poorer districts of industrial towns, where both communist and Nazi supporters were most numerous. It had little effect on the upper classes, so for the Bloch-Bauers life went on. It wasn't perfect, as the government evolved into what became known as Austrofascism, but it was a long way from conditions in Germany. The conservatives transformed the country into a one-party state and eliminated freedom of the press, but they were pro-business. There was anti-Semitism but mostly of the traditional Catholic type, and Viennese as influential as Ferdinand and Gustav had little to fear.

In summer 1937 the youngest of Maria's brothers, Robert, married. It was the first of two weddings in the family that year, because Maria herself had also found a partner. Frederik "Fritz" Altmann was 29, eight years older than she was, and came from another Viennese Jewish family. Altmann's mother had opened one of Vienna's first machine-knitting factories in the late 19th century. Her older son Bernhard saw the potential of the new knitting machines but thought his mother's business was too small, so in 1916 he set up his own in Switzerland. Two years later, while the war was still going on, he returned to Vienna and founded the Bernhard Altmann Knitting Mill. By the mid-1920s he had a chain of 40 small factories employing over 500 people, and when Fritz was seventeen he joined the company. Within a few years he'd traveled to the USA, Britain, Switzerland and even the USSR. Not long before he started work the Soviet government had invited Bernhard to open a knitting factory near Moscow, and Fritz was part or the team who went to Russia to manage it. He was impressed at how quickly the Soviet system could create infrastructure and a factory with 1,000 workers, but less amused a year later when they changed their minds, expelled the management and confiscated the factory.[viii]

In 1937, aged 29, Fritz met the 21-year-old Maria and they soon became close. Their respective families approved too, and in December they were married. It was, Fritz remembered, "the last happy wedding". He was right.

Since 1934 the government had been struggling with increasing desperation against pressure from Berlin. The Austrian Nazis were pushing strongly for unification, and Hitler was encouraging them, then attacking the Vienna regime for ignoring their "legitimate" demands. The first Austrofascist chancellor had been assassinated by Nazis during the failed 1934 coup; his replacement, Kurt Schuschnigg, began a policy of arresting and interning both Nazis and Social Democrats in an attempt to maintain stability, but it was a losing battle. In 1936 he signed the Germany-Austria Agreement, which he hoped would guarantee independence in exchange for the release of imprisoned Austrian Nazis and NSDAP representation in government, but it just encouraged Hitler to push harder. The two leaders met again in February 1938, where Hitler presented a new list of demands. The key one was that a strongly pro-unification Nazi be appointed as Minister of Public Security. Schuschnigg agreed, but when he returned to Vienna he made a last-ditch effort to break free of Berlin's influence. He announced the end of the one-party state, legalized the Social Democrats and called a referendum on Austrian independence for March 13.

Hitler wasn't impressed. He had already made his plans and fully intended to carry them out, so he simply rejected the Austrian moves. He declared that the referendum would be fraudulent and Germany wouldn't accept it; he wasn't willing to abandon ten million "Germans" who had the bad luck to live outside the Reich, so if Schuschnigg didn't hand over power to the Austrian Nazis by March 11 Germany would invade. Beaten, Schuschnigg resigned; next day the *Wehrmacht* entered Austria, where they were greeted with flowers.

But there were no flowers from Vienna's Jewish community. The worst excesses of the Nazi regime were still to come but persecutions had been underway in Germany within days of Hitler's ascension to power. Anti-Jewish laws restricted Jews' access to education, prohibited them from owning firearms and barred them from civil service jobs. In September 1935 The Nuremberg Laws stripped Germany's 500,000 Jews of their citizenship rights – voting or standing for office - and made it illegal for them to marry non-Jewish Germans; any previous mixed marriages were declared void. Their passports were stamped with a large Gothic letter J, making them valid to leave Germany but not to return. Even names were affected. Any German Jews with a name that wasn't identifiably Jewish had to adopt a middle name: "Israel" for men and "Sara" for women. As an example of spiteful discrimination it was hard to beat, even if in practice it was applied unevenly through the rest of the 1930s. While the senior Nazi leaders and ideologues were fanatical on the subject the anti-Semitism of many middle and lower ranking Party officials was much more lukewarm, and while few actively tried to assist Jewish former acquaintances they weren't always in a hurry to impose the worst of the laws. The writing was on the wall, though, and Jews began to leave Germany in large numbers. By the time the *Wehrmacht* rolled into Vienna nearly a quarter of a million had gone, mostly to the USA, UK and Palestine. They had made the right decision. Under constant pressure from the fanatics at the top, and the brown-uniformed street thugs at the bottom, the middle-ranking Party members who enforced the laws were becoming more zealous about doing so. And now the same bullying and oppression had come to Austria.

Jews in Vienna had been at risk of assault from the Nazi heavies who often roamed the streets looking for victims, but middle and upper-class Jews were usually less easy to recognize and didn't get as much trouble. With the Nazis now decisively in power that quickly began to change. Hitler announced his own referendum on Austrian independence, which was held on April 10. The results were overwhelmingly for unification with Germany, which wasn't too surprising. The ballot card had two circles, one marked Yes (for unification) and one No (for independence). In a less than subtle hint the Yes circle was twice the size of the other. There were no voting booths or ballot boxes either – voters had to mark their card in front of a Nazi official then hand it to him. This blatant intimidation was predictably effective. Some rural areas went ahead and voted in the officially cancelled referendum that Schuschnigg had organized, and most of the results were strongly against unification. In one village 95 percent voted for continued independence. When the Nazi referendum was held the same village was 73.3 percent in favor of union.[ix]

The world knew that the referendum was a sham, but enough Austrians did welcome the Nazis to muddy the waters. In any case there was nothing that could be done; the major European powers, Britain and France, were frantically rebuilding their militaries after years of neglect but weren't yet strong enough to challenge Hitler. In fact, when they finally did face the *Wehrmacht* in France two years later they were decisively defeated, and only the English Channel kept the Nazis from total domination of Europe. In 1938 it was hopeless to even think of opposing the takeover. Now, with Austria rapidly being absorbed as a province of the growing Reich, the Jews of Vienna were abandoned to their fate.

It didn't take long before the traditional Catholic anti-Semitism of Austria was displaced by the more virulent ideological strain promoted by the Nazis. Snobbery and social exclusion turned to vicious harassment and enforcement of the Nuremberg Laws, which now applied in Austria too. Within months of the Nazis taking power the new reign of terror began to affect the Bloch-Bauers. The first victim was Maria's brother Leopold.

Leopold had been watching events in Germany with alarm, and as soon as the German takeover began he urged his wife to flee with their son. On the night of April 12, as the German columns rolled into Austria, Antoinette and Peter drove to the border with the new state of Czechoslovakia. Leopold's fear had been well founded; the next day he was arrested by the *Geheime Staatspolizei* (Secret State Police) – the Gestapo. There was no evidence against him, of course, because he hadn't committed a crime, but that no longer mattered. One of the aims of the racial laws was to "Aryanize" Jewish businesses, which in practice meant confiscating them and handing them over to Party members. In any case Leopold's real crime was simply being a Jew, and in the Third Reich there was no defense against that charge. A surprising number of German and Austrian Jews managed to remain free, often quite openly, until the end of the war, but once one of them fell into the hands of the Gestapo there was usually no escape. Leopold Bloch-Bauer might have faced a rigged trial or that pretense might have been ignored, but either way the outcome would be the same – a concentration camp.

The Nazi security apparatus was split into two branches; one was the *Sicherheitsdienst*, or SD, which was the Nazis' own intelligence agency. It was responsible for operations outside Germany, including intelligence collecting and stirring up convenient trouble. The other branch was the security police, the SiPo, which itself was split into two sections. One of these was the *Kriminalpolizei*, the detective branch of the police,[1] and the other was the Gestapo. Both the intelligence and police branches answered to one of the most feared figures in Nazi Germany.

---

[1] All German police forces were unified and brought under the control of the SS in 1936.

Reinhard Heydrich was a former *Freikorps* member and naval officer who had joined the NSDAP in 1931 and was quickly recruited by Heinrich Himmler, who was busy setting up a Party counterintelligence service. After 1933 he rose quickly through the Nazi hierarchy and by summer 1938 he was one of the most powerful men in the regime. His SD agents had helped provoke the Anschluss and prepare lists of "undesirable" Austrians – including prominent Jews – to be detained. Later he helped organize the *Kristallnacht* pogrom and the early stages of the Holocaust, and masterminded persecution of Jews and other minorities in occupied Czechoslovakia. He was one of the 20th century's most ruthless and prolific criminals, and would undoubtedly have been executed after the war if Czech partisans hadn't assassinated him in 1942. In 1938, he had a social connection to the Bloch-Bauers, which earned him a minor place in family legend.

In the 1930s women weren't allowed to compete in many Olympic events, including most of the equestrian ones. However Leopold's wife was a world-class dressage rider who had often competed informally against German and Austrian Olympic competitors, many of whom were military and SS officers. One of them was Reinhard Heydrich. The secret police chief was a talented horseman who'd been awarded the German Equestrian Badge in gold, and Antoinette knew him through pre-Anschluss riding events. According to her son Peter a high-ranking Austrian friend – a Catholic – who knew of the connection approached Heydrich on her behalf.[x] The Austrian asked Heydrich, "Do you know who you have in jail?" He replied, "We've got a lot of people in jail." However, when he learned that one of them was the husband of someone he knew he made a strange decision. He had Leopold brought to him and offered him lunch, then told him to get out of the country by that night. Leopold and Antoinette took their son and all the valuables they could carry, and fled

Austria as fast as they could. They settled in Canada, where they changed their name to Bentley and founded a successful timber business.

As the threat of Nazi persecution loomed Vienna's Jews had already started thinking about escape. Many of them couldn't afford to leave; of those who could, some began selling what they could and heading for safer countries. It wasn't always easy to find a safe haven. Most countries were reluctant to open the doors to every refugee fleeing the Nazis, because it was already obvious that huge numbers of people could be affected. Some Jews aimed for Palestine but there was no guarantee of getting in there either. When the British had taken control of Palestine in 1919 around 90 percent of the population had been Muslim and Christian Arabs. By the late 1930s the Jewish population had almost doubled and the Arabs, worried about loss of their land, were becoming agitated. A revolt broke out in 1936 as discontented Arabs attacked settlers and the British police. In an attempt to ease the tensions, the British imposed a limit of 45,000 immigrants a year (later reduced to 15,000), which severely limited the options for escapees from Germany and Austria.

In any case the Zionist settlers in Palestine were mostly socialists from Poland and Ukraine, and the wealthy Bloch-Bauers and Altmanns had little interest in joining them. Instead they looked for options closer to home.

In late March, worried about the risk of a German takeover, Ferdinand had locked up his Vienna mansion and gone to his castle in Czechoslovakia. Now he was safe from arrest or harassment, but under the Nuremberg Laws he couldn't legally return to Austria – trying to get back to Vienna almost guaranteed the Gestapo would get him. Antoinette's father Otto Pick went to Switzerland. Karl emigrated to Paris, where he married in May 1940 before fleeing to Canada days later as the Germans invaded France. Bernhard Altmann also fled to France. His brother and Maria, however, were more optimistic. They shouldn't have been, because there was more to the Nazis' persecution than their insane racial ideology. They were also heavily motivated by greed.

Chapter 5: Stolen Treasure

Peter Bentley's story of his father's lunch with
Heydrich may have been true, but even if it was
there was a lot more to the story. Leopold Bloch-
Bauer had spent nine days in a Gestapo cell
before being released; he was freed on March
23 but he didn't leave Austria that night. In fact
he was forbidden to leave. Almost two months
later a Viennese banker, who may have been a
Gestapo agent, visited his father-in-law in Zurich.
Switzerland was a neutral country but many of
its German-speaking citizens were pro-Nazi and
the Gestapo could operate freely there. The
banker, Doctor H. Mann, told Pick that if he
surrendered his assets to the bank Leopold
would be allowed to leave the country.[xi]

Unsurprisingly Pick agreed to the extortion demand, and signed the bulk of his money over to Mann's bank. On May 31 Leopold was allowed to fly to Switzerland after paying a "flight tax". He then rejoined Antoinette and Peter, and together they traveled first to Britain then on to Canada.

On July 2 Maria's father Gustav died aged 76, leaving his estate to his wife Therese. Gustav hadn't owned a business the Nazis were interested in, but he did have other treasures. One of his most prized possessions was a Stradivarius cello he'd been given by the Rothschilds, which was regularly used at family parties. In mid-June the Gestapo confiscated it; Maria always said that her father died of a broken heart after this loss.[xii]

With Gustav's death many of the family's remaining assets in Vienna – including Ferdinand's art collection – were left without their last protector. Meanwhile the Nazis continued trying to seize control of Jewish-owned businesses, sometimes manipulating the law to create an appearance of legality and sometimes resorting to simple thuggery. A manufactured tax evasion case was brought against ÖZAG; Ferdinand, still in Czechoslovakia, was helpless to prevent the company being seized. Then the Nazis turned their attention to the Altmann knitwear business.

The owner of the company was Bernhard Altmann, who was safe in France. His brother and sister-in-law were still in Vienna though, and they could be exploited. In June Fritz Altmann was arrested and sent to the concentration camp at Dachau in Bavaria. Maria was placed under house arrest in Vienna.

Dachau was the first of the Nazi concentration camps; it opened in March 1933, only weeks after Hitler took power. It was originally built to hold political prisoners, mainly communists and Social Democrats, but as persecution of Jews increased they began to be sent there as well. Before the war and the initiation of the Final Solution conditions in the camp were harsh, but the difference between Dachau and most countries' prisons was one of degree. Later, between 1942 and 1945, over 30,000 people died at Dachau but in 1938 it was simply an extremely strict prison camp. The inmates were forced to work in a munitions factory, and because it was the first of the camps it functioned as a training school for camp guards. Between 1935 and 1939 Dachau was also the center of a massive extortion industry. Before the outbreak of war around 11,000 German, Austrian and Czech Jews were imprisoned there. After a few weeks of the brutal camp routine they would then be offered the chance to emigrate, on condition that they "voluntarily" donated their assets to the Reich. Those who signed over their homes and businesses to the SS were released and allowed to leave the Reich; the others, the ones who refused to cooperate or had nothing of value, stayed behind the wire. After 1941 they were transferred to the extermination camps in the east.

Fritz Altmann didn't have a business, but his brother Bernhard did and the Nazis wanted it. Their methods were cynical in the extreme – Bernhard had the company ownership papers and share certificates, but the Nazis had Fritz and Maria. They offered him a simple choice through their agents in France – either sign over the company or Fritz would stay in the camp. Bernhard considered his options, and realized they were limited. He couldn't return to Vienna to run the company anyway, so it was worthless to him. On the other hand by signing it away he could perhaps buy freedom for Fritz and Maria. It can't have been an easy decision but finally he accepted the demand and signed over the company. In return the Gestapo released Fritz from Dachau. He was reunited with Maria and the couple fled, first to Holland and then through Liverpool and, by ship, to the USA. They settled in Fall River, Massachusetts and started trying to rebuild their lives.

Meanwhile Austria served as a springboard for the next stage of Hitler's expansionist plans. When the Austro-Hungarian Empire had fractured in 1918 the new states hadn't formed perfectly along ethnic lines, and the border districts of Czechoslovakia were mostly populated by German speakers. Now Hitler began stirring up nationalist unrest in this region, the Sudetenland. The crisis quickly escalated and after a series of conferences the French and British governments, who hadn't yet fully rearmed and were desperate to ensure at least another year of peace, agreed on September 15 that the Sudetenland should be transferred to Germany. The government of Czechoslovakia wasn't even invited to the talks.

Unfortunately for Ferdinand Bloch-Bauer his summer home, the castle where he'd taken refuge, was in the Sudetenland. He was forced to flee again, this time to Switzerland. The Vienna Jewish community, a key part of the city's society for centuries, had been scattered and irreparably broken. Its members were in camps or in exile, and most of their property was now pillaged by the Nazis. Ferdinand's Bohemian summer castle was appropriated by Heydrich himself as a vacation home. His Vienna mansion was converted into offices for the propaganda ministry and the rail service, the *Reichsbahn*. Then the plunderers turned their attention to smaller items.

From Hitler's point of view the aim of all this looting was to help finance the expansion of the military for the war he knew was coming. Many of his subordinates, however, grabbed the chance to enrich themselves in the process. The most notorious example is air force chief Hermann Göring, who collected more than 2,000 paintings and other pieces of art, but it's likely that even larger numbers of works were stolen by low-level officials. When a Nazi lawyer was appointed to liquidate Ferdinand's estate the results were predictable. Dr. Erich Fuerher found buyers for Ferdinand's porcelain collection, his antique furniture and most of his art, but he picked out a handful of paintings for himself. Hitler had very strong views about modern art, preferring traditional realistic landscapes and portraits, but Fuerher seems to have been more progressive in his tastes. Among the works he chose were all five of Ferdinand's Klimts.[xiii]

What happened next confused the issue for the next 60 years. Fuerher made a deal with the Austrian Gallery to exchange two of the works for a painting Ferdinand had donated to the Belvedere in 1936. The Klimts he offered were *Apfelbaum I* and *Portrait of Adele Bloch-Bauer I* – the golden portrait. The gallery eagerly accepted, and Fuerher delivered the two paintings along with a note. The note stated that the paintings were being given to the Belvedere in accordance with the last will and testament of Adele Bloch-Bauer.[xiv] There was just enough truth in the note to muddy the waters.

Later, in 1943, Fuehrer sold two more of the Klimts. *Adele Bloch-Bauer II* went to the Belvedere and another to the Vienna City Gallery. The final one stayed in his personal collection. Eventually, all five of the paintings were transferred to the Austrian Gallery, where they would remain for decades.

Chapter 6: Rebuilding

When Fritz Altmann was released from Dachau he found himself and Maria still trapped in the Reich while officials considered his request to emigrate. On the positive side he was no longer in a concentration camp and had been reunited with Maria, but now they were both under house arrest in Berlin.[xv] With nothing left to offer as a bribe they would have little chance of a second release, so it was vital to escape to a free country as soon as possible. Luckily Bernhard Altmann was still in France, and the brothers began working on a plan.

Today, the borders between central and western European nations have been removed, and people can travel freely around most of the continent. In 1938 it was different. Customs posts sat on every road that crossed a border; officers boarded trains at the station before the border and checked all passengers' papers. Between crossing points there were fences, usually patrolled by paramilitary forces. Maria and Fritz didn't have the exit stamps that would let them leave by road or rail, so unless they felt like waiting for the Nazis to make up their minds their only option was to dodge the patrols and get through the border fence. They didn't want to escape to Poland, Czechoslovakia or anywhere else in Eastern Europe – it was already obvious the Nazis had ambitions in that direction – and Italy was ruled by Hitler's Fascist allies. They could probably get into Switzerland but that would leave them surrounded by the Reich. That left France, Belgium and the Netherlands as possible destinations. However, the border with France was one of the most militarized in the world, defended by the huge (but useless) fortresses of the Maginot Line and heavily patrolled by the French army. Finally they decided on the Netherlands, and Bernhard traveled to Amsterdam to make arrangements.

The first step was to get out of Berlin. One night Maria told their guards that Fritz needed to see a dentist urgently. Lulled by the couple's good behavior up to that point the policemen let them go, but it was a ruse – the Altmanns disappeared into the night and fled west, towards the Dutch border. They knew the Gestapo would soon be contacting every police and railway station in Germany but they didn't need much time. They outsmarted their pursuers by catching the morning flight to Cologne; then, the next night – before the hunt could really get under way – a friendly farmer led them to the border fence under cover of darkness.[xvi] It was nothing like the Inner German Border of the Cold War, just a fence with a few strands of barbed wire on top, and it wasn't too difficult to climb. Maria tore a stocking on the barbs as she swung over the top – she kept that stocking as a memento for the rest of her life.

From the Netherlands the couple made their way to Liverpool, in England, and at first considered staying there. Bernhard knew Sir Frederick Marquis, a British businessman who as Lord Woolton later became famous as the wartime Minister of Food, and this was a huge help. At first the Altmanns were in a difficult position because Fritz and Maria had come to Britain without passports, and Marquis was able to sort this out. He then persuaded Liverpool city council to give Bernhard a new building, where he immediately opened another knitwear factory.[xvii]

Then, in September 1939, the Second World War began. The Nazis had already seized the rest of Czechoslovakia in March; now they and the USSR invaded Poland. There was a brief quiet period, and then in May 1940 the *Wehrmacht* invaded the Netherlands, Belgium and France. Within six weeks France had fallen and the Germans were at the English Channel. While the British dug in and grimly prepared to fight to the death, many of the refugees who had fled from the continent were convinced that invasion was inevitable. They feared that yet again they would find themselves trapped inside the expanding Reich, and many of them fled once more. The Altmanns were among them.

In summer 1940 Maria and Fritz arrived in Massachusetts, where they settled briefly in Fall River. Once a major center of textile production this city must have seemed the perfect place, but the clothing industry had been seriously damaged by the Great Depression and turned out to be in terminal decline. A year later they moved on again, this time to Los Angeles. Months later, the USA joined the war too.

Fritz, a qualified engineer, soon found himself a job with Lockheed Aircraft at Burbank. At the same time he and Maria settled down to what they hoped would be a normal family life at last. Their first son was born in 1942; three more children followed by 1957.

As the war went on it became clear that Europe was never going to be the same again. While Bernhard still hoped to return to Austria one day and reclaim whatever remained of his business, Maria and Fritz were more reluctant. Finally they decided it would be better to remain in California, where they already felt more at home. In 1945 they became naturalized US citizens. On November 13 the same year Ferdinand Bloch-Bauer died, nearly penniless, in Zürich. Before he died he made a new will, leaving what remained of his assets to Maria and her siblings.[xviii]

\#   \#   \#

As he had planned, Bernhard Altmann returned to Vienna after the war, now that Austria was an independent country again. He found the knitwear factories almost undamaged, although the occupying Soviets had stolen much of the machinery. The Nazi seizure of the business had been voided so he was able to install new machines and restart production. By 1947 the business had become Austria's largest exporter, and Bernhard had persuaded Fritz to give up his job with Lockheed and return to the textile industry. High quality knitwear was very popular in the postwar period, especially cashmere sweaters, and to meet demand the Altmanns opened a factory in San Antonio, Texas. Despite having no previous business experience Maria also joined the company; Fritz found her help invaluable.

Bernhard Altmann died in 1960, and without him at the helm the business quickly fell apart. The premises in Austria were repossessed by the banks, while the company name and Texas plant were sold to a US garment company. Fritz and Maria opened their own business importing ladies' suits from Italy and Hong Kong, and while the first few years were a struggle they eventually managed to build it up into a prosperous company. Before long Maria had spun off her own business, too, and was running a fashionable Hollywood boutique. Eventually her success overtook her husband's, and Fritz wound up his own company to join hers.

#   #   #

When Fritz died in 1994 Maria, now aged 78, had enough money left to see her through a comfortable retirement. After an eventful life in which she'd mingled with the cream of European society, fled from the Nazis in a daring midnight escape and built a successful new life on a different continent she though the excitement was finally over and she could grow old in peace, surrounded by her four children. She was wrong.

Chapter 7: Openness

The industrial-scale art theft perpetrated by the Nazis was no secret, but returning the spoils to its rightful owners was far from simple. Many owners of confiscated works had died in the extermination camps or pogroms in the occupied east, and often no surviving heirs could be found. More had disappeared into the famously secretive Swiss banks – hundreds of paintings may lie in deposit boxes belonging to Nazis who are themselves long dead. The situation in Austria was nowhere near as murky as in Switzerland but it was still complicated. At the end of the war the country had been occupied by the Soviets, who wanted to bring it into their sphere of influence, but after long negotiations between the four allies it was finally given its independence back in 1955. The government immediately declared neutrality, and Austria stayed as far away from the Cold War as possible. Both sides used it alternately as neutral ground and the launch pad for intelligence operations against each other, and the Austrians themselves became very cautious and defensive. This bred a conservative approach to life that partly insulated the country from the social progress underway in Western Europe, and, rather than confronting the events of 1938-1945, most Austrians preferred to leave them buried in the past.

Then, after the fall of the Berlin Wall in 1990, Vienna started to come under increasing pressure to investigate the crimes of the Nazi authorities. There was little enthusiasm for the process, because most Austrians were wary of unearthing the stories that lay behind the country's vanished Jews and the artworks that had appeared in the country's museums and galleries since 1938. Not everyone was so hesitant, however, and in 1998 the Green Party managed to push a bill through parliament that forced the government, and more importantly state-owned collections, to cooperate with investigations into the real ownership of the country's art treasures. For one man, investigative journalist Hubertus Czernin, this was just the opportunity he'd been waiting for.

Czernin had a reputation for not being afraid of scandal; he'd already investigated claims of child abuse in the Catholic Church, which in the 1990s were still being denied by the Vatican. Now he suspected another cover-up, this time involving the sudden flood of art that Austrian galleries had acquired in the late 1930s. The new law allowed him to demand access to the records of the Belvedere, the first journalist to be allowed to study them, and it wasn't long before he started to find clear evidence that much of what had been looted from Austrian and Czech Jews had found its way, through one channel or another, into state-owned collections. Of course much of this wasn't surprising; it had been known for decades that some works had dubious histories. However, Czernin started to wonder exactly how large the problem was and decided to do some digging into paintings that, officially, had been donated. He set his sights high, and started investigating the Belvedere's collection of Klimts.

Straight away he knew he'd hit journalistic gold. In the files relating to *Adele Bloch-Bauer I* was Dr. Fuerher's note stating that he was delivering the painting to the gallery "in accordance with the last will of Adele Bloch-Bauer". But Czernin knew Adele hadn't actually owned the painting and that the Belvedere had acquired it years before Ferdinand's death. Like everyone else he'd believed Ferdinand had given the paintings to the Belvedere himself, but now he had proof they'd been handed over by a Nazi lawyer long after Ferdinand himself had left the country. Tracing Ferdinand's will he soon found that his estate had gone to his nieces and nephews and that the Klimts – it didn't take much more work to find the others had also come to the gallery via Fuerher – should have been included.

When she heard the news Maria was astonished. She remembered the painting, but she had also assumed Ferdinand had donated it to the gallery in accordance with Adele's last wishes. Now, suddenly, she found that her uncle's Klimts should have been inherited by her and her siblings – and now she was the only one of Ferdinand's heirs left alive.

Maria was now 82, and her only real interest in the paintings was that they would allow her to leave a valuable inheritance for her own children. She spoke to some art experts who confirmed that any one of the Klimts would be worth millions of dollars, but that the golden portrait of Adele was by far the most valuable. Maria decided that the three landscapes would be enough to provide for her and her children, and approached the Austrian government with an offer; if they returned the landscapes she was happy for them to keep the two portraits of her aunt. Given the relative values of the paintings it was an extremely generous suggestion and Maria expected that Vienna would accept immediately, but she – and the Austrians – had miscalculated. Unused to public scrutiny of their art collections, the government didn't take her suggestion seriously. They had the paintings, they had been in the state gallery for decades and they didn't see why they should hand any of them over to an old woman in California. She wrote several letters asking for either compensation or the return of the landscapes, but Austria simply refused to discuss the issue.[xix] It's possible the Austrian government believed Maria was too old to pursue a case against them. If so, they had badly underestimated her. She had made a generous offer and been rudely rebuffed; now she took a harder line, and decided to get all five paintings back. With Vienna refusing to cooperate it was obviously going to take legal action to recover the paintings, so she turned first to the Austrian courts. There she found a surprising obstacle.

Almost any civil suit requires a filing fee to be paid before it can move forward. This is a controversial issue, with some campaigners arguing it reduces access to justice, but in the USA, the cost isn't usually prohibitive. In Arizona, it can be as low as $17, while in some states it runs to around $500. The higher fees can be painful, but they rarely actually prevent anyone from filing. The Austrian system is different though; the filing fee is a percentage of the sum the plaintiff is trying to recover. That's not a big deal if the case is over an unpaid bill for $500, but the property Maria wanted back was five original Klimt masterpieces with a total value estimated at over $135 million. When she tried to file a suit against the government she was told the fee to initiate the case would be over €1 million – around $1.6 million at the time.

There was no way Maria could afford such a high fee, and even the Austrian court recognized that it was unreasonable; they lowered the fee to $350,000. Unfortunately, even that was too much, especially as the Austrian government immediately appealed the reduction,[xx] and she gave up on the idea of going to court in Vienna. She was still determined to see justice done, though, and asked a lawyer friend if there was any way to bring the case before a US court. Randol Schoenberg believed the case was probably unwinnable but he agreed to look anyway. The relevant law was the 1976 Foreign Sovereign Immunities Act, which formalized the old principle that citizens couldn't sue a foreign government in a US court. It seems obvious – after all, an American court has no jurisdiction in Vienna, and Austria could simply ignore any ruling – but that's never stopped people trying. The first recorded case was in 1812, when the owners of a Baltimore schooner that had been captured by the French tried to sue Napoleon Bonaparte to get it back. Finally, during the Ford administration, the government decided it was time to provide some guidance to cut down the number of unworkable cases being put forward and the FSIA was passed. The new law was remarkably simple. The burden of proof was on the defendant to prove that they were a foreign state but if they could do so – which would be easy enough for the government of Austria – they were immune from prosecution in any US court unless a statutory exemption applied. Schoenberg's initial reaction was that the law was clear and the case was unwinnable, but out of curiosity he checked the statutory exemptions. Most of them were clearly irrelevant; this wasn't an admiralty case, the Austrians weren't likely to voluntarily waive immunity and they hadn't committed a tort in the USA. The case didn't involve hostage-taking and it didn't relate to commercial activity. But then he found clause § 1605(a)(5).

§ 1605(a)(5) creates an exemption from sovereign immunity where a state has seized property in violation of international law. The destruction of Austria's Jewish community had certainly been a violation of international law and the confiscation of property had been part of that process, so Schoenberg realized that he might have found a way to justify a case. The only problem was timing; the Klimts had been confiscated in 1938, but the FSIA didn't become law until 1976. Everything would depend on whether a court ruled the law applied retroactively, and Article 1 of the United States Constitution forbids *ex post facto* – after the fact – lawmaking. Still, Altmann agreed it was worth a shot. Schoenberg resigned from his law firm and began working on the case full time.[xxi]

The case was launched in the US District Court for Central California in 2000 (where the filing fee was only $400) and used the FSIA as a key argument. Representatives of the Austrian government argued against the validity of the case, stating that there was nothing in the FSIA to say it could be applied retroactively, but the District Court disagreed. There was also nothing in the Act to say it couldn't be applied retroactively, they pointed out, nor was there any indication that when Congress passed the FSIA they intended it to have limited reach. The court ruled in Maria's favor, but following an appeal the case was passed to the US Supreme Court. That hearing began on February 25, 2004 with arguments from Schoenberg, the Austrian government and the Belvedere. The Austrians' main argument was that applying the FSIA retroactively would impose costs on them that would not have been incurred under US law as it existed in 1945, when their sovereignty was restored. On the surface it was a compelling argument, and it had some support from the

1994 *Landgraf v. USI Film Products* case which had ruled against retroactivity. When Chief Justice William Rehnquist stood up to deliver the verdict on June 4, 2004 the entire legal profession was wondering what he was going to say and what new cases it would open up for them.

The decision the court had reached was one that Rehnquist himself did not support. The Austrian argument was rejected; the FSIA did not create any new laws, the court had decided, but simply clarified the existing laws the USA had been operating under since 1812 or earlier. Of the nine justices three, including Rehnquist, disagreed – but the remaining six carried the day, and the ruling was that Maria Altmann had the right to sue the Austrian government in a US district court.

Rather than face an American court the Austrian government finally agreed to arbitration, to be held at their own supreme court in Vienna. They probably saw this as a compromise that would give them a chance of a better deal, but for Maria the time for compromising was past. She was now determined to recover all five paintings. The Austrians were equally determined to keep them and they had huge public support – the paintings, especially *Adele Bloch-Bauer I*, were regarded as national treasures. However, the opinion of the government and public wasn't important; what mattered was the panel of three judges who would hear the arguments of each side.

The government's case was actually very weak; they were still arguing that the paintings had been donated through Adele's will, and that they had made a concession by allowing Ferdinand to keep them during his lifetime. There was too much evidence against them, though. The records Czernin had discovered proved that they had been "donated" by the Nazi lawyer Fuerher, and not by Ferdinand. It was also established that Ferdinand actually had donated a sixth Klimt to the Belvedere before the Anschluss, in 1936; if he had intended to donate all six he would almost certainly have made some mention of it at this time. The panel also didn't think it likely that he would have given his most valuable paintings to a regime that was busily persecuting him and the entire Jewish community he had spent his life in. Finally there was the question of ownership: had the paintings even been Adele's to give?

It's likely the judges would have ruled the way they did anyway, but in the end it was the last point that settled it. The panel reached their decision in January 2006. The paintings, they said, had been the property of Ferdinand Bloch-Bauer, not his wife. The wording of Adele's will implied that she was asking Ferdinand to donate the Klimts, not ordering the donation herself. Ferdinand clearly had chosen not to follow Adele's wish. Therefore, they announced, the five paintings were to be turned over to Maria.

Chapter 8: Justice

The decision caused uproar in Austria, and the
blame was placed squarely on the government.
As the Belvedere announced a final brief
exhibition, advertised with the slogan *Adele Geht*
– "Adele is leaving" – the Austrian people
vigorously condemned their political leaders for
not coming to an arrangement with Maria earlier.
If they had paid more attention to her first
approaches, and treated her seriously, they
could have given her the valuable but less
renowned landscapes and kept the two portraits.
Now, one of the greatest ever created in Austria,
was leaving the country.

For Maria, meanwhile, a great historic wrong had been righted. She always insisted it hadn't been about the money but now she had to decide what to do with the paintings. By now she was 90 years old, and her priority was passing on what she could to her children; the best way to do that, she decided, was to sell the Klimts and leave the money to them. The paintings arrived in Los Angeles in March 2006, under heavy security – wild rumors about their possible sale price were already circulating. First, though, they were exhibited again, at the Los Angeles County Museum of Art on Wiltshire Boulevard. That was a sensible decision, for practical as well as cultural reasons. The museum's own collection included many extremely valuable works and their security was state of the art. The Klimts were safer there than anywhere else Maria could have arranged. They stayed on display until late June; then they were transferred to the New York branch of the Christie's auction house.

As it turned out only four of the paintings were actually auctioned. *Adele Bloch-Bauer I* was sold privately in early July. The buyer was Ronald Lauder, a Republican politician and prominent Jewish activist who is also an heir to the Estée Lauder cosmetics fortune. He was willing to spend a good slice of his multi-billion dollar fortune on art – although the price for the sale was never officially revealed it's rumored that he paid $135 million for *Adele*, the highest price ever commanded by any painting until Picasso's *Le Réve* sold for $155 million seven years later. Many wealthy collectors like to keep their art away from the public eye, but in 2001 Lauder had opened the *Neue Galerie* on New York's Fifth Avenue. The centerpiece of the gallery is its collection of early 20th century German and Austrian art, so it was the perfect place for his new purchase – *Adele I* has been on display there since July 13, 2006.

The next painting to be sold was *Adele Bloch-Bauer II*. This was auctioned in November the same year and finally went for $87.9 million.[xxii] The three landscapes made another $114.7 million between them; in all Maria earned over $330 million from the Klimts. After settling Schoenberg's 40 percent fee that still left her with $200 million, which she divided among her children.

Chapter 9: Death and Legacy

Maria was delighted at the outcome of the case. The paintings themselves had little value to her and her only interest in the money was as an inheritance for her family – her own lifestyle didn't change at all after her victory. Instead, she explained, it was about seeing that the right thing was done no matter how late in the day. "I persisted," she said, "out of a desire that Austria should see that there is such a thing as justice." A common complaint among victims of the Nazi oppression has been that Austria has portrayed itself as a sufferer, too, when in fact Austrians were deeply involved in the Reich's atrocities. Cynics joke that Austria's greatest achievement has been to convince the world that Hitler was German. Perhaps Maria's struggle for justice helped to break down this defensive attitude, though. After all, the US courts only ruled that she was free to sue; it was an Austrian tribunal that returned her family's property to her.

Maria herself took a realistic view of the case.
Asked if she felt sorry for the Austrians, she
laughed. They had made no effort to
compensate the family over the decades they'd
held the paintings, and had ignored her in 1999
when she offered a guarantee that the paintings
wouldn't leave the country if ownership was
returned to her.[xxiii] Instead they'd been stubborn,
and now they had only themselves to blame.

By the time the Klimts were sold and the funds distributed, Altmann was exhausted and in failing health. Her personality was as lively as ever, though. In early 2008 she started looking for a new caregiver and settled on actor Gregor Collins, who was between jobs and had been persuaded to apply for the position by a friend. At first Collins was reluctant, but soon found himself captivated by her energy. Soon he found himself sitting fascinated for hours a day as Maria told him stories of her life in Vienna before the war, her escape from the Gestapo and the struggle to build a new life in California. As hard as it is to believe for anyone who knows actors, he once told a director he wouldn't be able to meet him to discuss a part because he had plans to go out with Maria.[xxiv]

Maria Altmann died in Los Angeles on February 7, 2011, just eleven days short of her 95th birthday. Her death marked the final passing of the Viennese society that had been so brutally disrupted by Hitler, but her life had played a major part in making the Austrian government finally face up to its responsibilities to the victims of Nazism. In her last decade she was often in the news, and she was featured in three documentaries about the case. From now on, as long as the Bloch-Bauer Klimts are exhibited and admired, the story of Maria and her fight to liberate them will be part of the paintings' history. The museums of Europe, North America and the Pacific Rim still contain many works of art that were acquired under dubious circumstances but the case brought by Maria removed one of the last obstacles to making amends for the systematic theft perpetrated between 1933 and 1945. It also set legal precedents that go far beyond the trade in stolen art, and make it far harder for criminals to gain immunity through the passage of time. It was a remarkable end to a remarkable life.

[i] Penck, S. & Weidinger, A. (2014); *Gustav Klimt: Life and Work*
[ii] Penck, S. & Weidinger, A. (2014); *Gustav Klimt: Life and Work*
[iii] Partsch, S. (1989); *Klimt: Life and Work*
[iv] Hitler, A. (1929); *Mein Kampf*
[v] Kershaw, I. (1999); *Hitler: 1889-1936:Hubris*
[vi] Esaak, S; *The Bloch-Bauer Klimts*
   http://arthistory.about.com/od/klim1/a/blochbauerklimt.htm
[vii] Kershaw, I. (2008); *Hitler: A Biography*
[viii] Geni.com; *Fritz Altmann*
   http://www.geni.com/people/Fritz-
Altmann/6000000008354887264
[ix] Tirol Multimedial; *Anschluss Tirols an NS-Deutschland und Judenpogrom in Innsbruck 1938*
   http://www.tirolmultimedial.at/tmm/themen/0705v.html
[x] RealEstate.ca (Sep 22, 2005); *Two of Vancouver's oldest mansions changes hands this month*
   http://www.6717000.com/blog/2005/09/two-of-vancouvers-
oldest-mansions-changes-hands-this-month/
[xi] Holocaust Claims Resolution Tribunal, *In re Account of Österreichische Zuckerindustrie AG Syndicate, Exhibit C*
[xii] Daily Telegraph (Feb 8, 2011); *Obituary – Maria Altmann*

http://www.telegraph.co.uk/news/obituaries/8311944/Maria-
Altmann.html
[xiii] Altmann v. Republic of Austria; *Maria V Altmann Case re: Bloch-Bauer paintings*
   http://www.lootedart.com/MFEU4R18009_print;Y
[xiv] Altmann v. Republic of Austria; *Maria V Altmann Case re: Bloch-Bauer paintings*
   http://www.lootedart.com/MFEU4R18009_print;Y

[xv] Daily Express (Jul 27, 2014); *Helen Mirren in BBC Nazi art theft drama*

http://www.express.co.uk/entertainment/tv-radio/491883/Helen-Mirren-to-play-Maria-Altmann-in-BBC-biopic

[xvi] New York Times (Feb 9, 2011); *Maria Altmann, Pursuer of Family's Stolen Paintings, Dies at 94*

http://www.nytimes.com/2011/02/09/arts/design/09altmann.html?_r=0

[xvii] Geni.com; *Fritz Altmann*

http://www.geni.com/people/Fritz-Altmann/6000000008354887264

[xviii] New York Times (Feb 9, 2011); *Maria Altmann, Pursuer of Family's Stolen Paintings, Dies at 94*

http://www.nytimes.com/2011/02/09/arts/design/09altmann.html?_r=0

[xix] Daily Express (Jul 27, 2014); *Helen Mirren in BBC Nazi art theft drama*

http://www.express.co.uk/entertainment/tv-radio/491883/Helen-Mirren-to-play-Maria-Altmann-in-BBC-biopic

[xx] *REPUBLIC OF AUSTRIA V. ALTMANN (03-13) 541 U.S. 677 (2004)*

[xxi] Pacific Lutheran University, *A quest for justice and the return of lost masterpieces*

http://www.plu.edu/news/2012/11/holocaust-lecture/home.php

[xxii] Esaak, S; *The Bloch-Bauer Klimts*

http://arthistory.about.com/od/klim1/a/blochbauerklimt.htm

[xxiii] Daily Express (Jul 27, 2014); *Helen Mirren in BBC Nazi art theft drama*

http://www.express.co.uk/entertainment/tv-radio/491883/Helen-Mirren-to-play-Maria-Altmann-in-BBC-biopic

[xxiv] Collins, G. (2012); *The Accidental Caregiver*

CPSIA information can be obtained
at www.ICGtesting.com
Printed in the USA
LVHW08s1800111018
593271LV00011B/468/P

9 781502 954787